HITCHHIKING

-

Feel The Good Vibrations

by
Liam Browne

2019

www.liambrowne.com

Some names have been changed to protect the privacy of family and friends.

Copyright © Liam Browne 2019
All rights reserved
This book or any portion thereof may not be reproduced or used in any manner whatsoever without the express written permission of the author except for the use of brief quotations in line with copyright law.

Cover Art by Matt Crump
Photography by Lucy Reynolds
Cover Design by Paulo Kevin Duelli
Edited by Johanna Craven
Proofread & Formatted by Evelyn Kristen Hills

Always for you, Mum

A FREE 'UNPUBLISHED' POEM FOR YOU!

As a massive thank you for buying this book I would like to give you a little present. This is only for you, the people who have supported my work. I hope my experience has opened your mind to trying things you thought were not possible.

This is a poem about perception and social conditioning. A poem about drugs and alcohol and dogma. A poem about doing what feels right in your heart and not what other people and organisations say is right for you. Steps into your own power. Be all that you can be!

Magnificence is waiting around the corner. Move beyond you imagined limitations.

You can download 'DEALER WITH IT' at:
www.liambrowne.com/dealerwithit.

Feel the Good Vibrations
England & Scotland
2013

With my girlfriend having loads of crazy stuff going on over the coming weeks, I decided I would go on a hitchhiking tour of the UK.

I'd just come back from eight months in the Americas and hitchhiking had led me to have some mind-blowing experiences. I'd met some amazing people. I really wanted to try it out at home.

I thought, "How would this work in Britain? Is it possible? Do people still do it? And would anyone pick me up?" I had no idea of the answers to any of these questions. I just put my faith in the Universe.

I set off on my UK tour to see friends who were dotted about the country, testing out the generosity of the British public and seeing where the wind would blow me. I felt that arriving home to Manchester after stops in Buckinghamshire, Rothwell, Newcastle, Glasgow and Lancaster would bring my travels to a harmonious end and deliver the final chapter to what had been an epic adventure.

I remembered in the 80s as a kid, I would see people hitchhiking all the time with their little cardboard signs, their destination scribbled in marker pen at every entrance to a motorway. They typically looked like punks, rockers and homeless people with flamboyant haircuts and coloured jackets. We never picked them up. We would drive past, and I would stare at them through the window wondering where they were going, why they didn't have a car and why they had mad hair.

I decided I would stick to the hitchhiking style I had adopted on my travels, slight bend in the hip with my thumb sticking out in the direction I was going. It had worked perfectly in America; how could I go wrong?

For the life of me, I couldn't think of the last time I had seen a hitchhiker whilst travelling around Britain. Why had it died out? Were we not as kind as drivers anymore? Were people too scared to hitch and drivers too scared to pick up hitchers or did everyone own a car now? Or was there some Government, business and media conspiracy to make people comply with how things should be? Regardless, I was doing it. Failure or difficulty never entered my mind.

After leaving my girlfriend, Fhian, I headed for my French "mum's" house in Bourne End, Buckinghamshire. This was where I would begin my hitchhiking.

I spent two blissful days with Red and Laurence in their thatched-roofed, perfect picturesque home. It's actually up there with my favourite pieces of property in the world, and the homely feel they create is, well, well homely.

A huge paddock runs parallel with the long drive, (me working classmates would call it a football pitch) and then three garages that are bigger than most people's houses sit at the front of the house. All with their matching thatched roofs. Open old-style coach house doors lead to the front door, and the majesty of this stylish home is revealed.

It was so good to be with Laurence and feel that motherly energy she had so kindly given me since my own mother's death. It was nice to sleep in the same bed for two nights and be in such elegant surroundings, even though my traveller attire was not very fitting and the musty smell of me hair upset Laurence a little bit.

She dropped me off at a place we should not have stopped at. It was on the A404 road that leads onto the M40. There was a lay-by, so I just kind of dived out, kissed Laurence goodbye and looked at the traffic coming off the A404 onto the slip road at about 50 miles an hour.

I thought, 'Wow, I will be lucky if someone stops'.

I was about to pop my British hitchhiking cherry. I know Laurence thought I was mental to be hitchhiking and so did most people I'd told about this recent expedition. The most common reaction was, "Can you still do that?" But since I'd returned from the Amazon, I felt like I was the light, I could achieve anything, go anywhere, meet the people I needed to meet and be constantly supported. All would be provided because I was so open and so in love with everything. My energy felt so pure, and I thought everything would work out perfectly.

I assumed my position, instantly realising (OH NO) everything was in reverse; the cars were going a different way. I was using me left thumb instead of my durable right that had been an ever-present in my automotive lift-sharing pursuits so far. I put out the left thumb, it hung low, no muscle memory or strength in my forearm to hold it up, so I opted for my right arm across my stomach and two fingers to support my flailing left arm. I stood there with cars flying by me thinking an accident may be caused if anyone did stop and wondered if this was even possible and legal. Would I be arrested soon?

I was on my way to my friends Sally and Phil's who lived in a small town called Rothwell near Kettering. I walked a little further, so people had more time to see me. The next thing I knew, a van pulled up, and I was being whisked down the M40 towards Oxford.

Wijchik was my driver, and he wasn't going massively far, but it was a quick start. He was a Polish bloke in England to earn money to take home and build a house. He was working for a garden centre delivering plants, his contract stipulating that he could pick up nicely dressed hitchhikers.

He dropped me a little while from Oxford on this really quiet spot. I was struggling to imagine getting picked up there because a car only went past every few minutes. I said my mantra, as I did every morning:

'I call upon the highest vibrational energy to come through me now. I call upon all my chakras to be open and active now. I ask the Divine's love to come through me now and settle within my heart chakra. I am grateful to be at the perfect place on my spiritual path. I am open to all the opportunities given to me by my guides for my highest good. I am grateful to be of service to God and humanity. I am open to receive all the abundance given to me by the Divine to help me continue on my spiritual path. I am worthy of being abundant. I know how to be abundant. Being abundant makes me happy. Being on my spiritual path and working with the Divine makes me so happy and brings me so much joy. I would like to plant this seed of happiness within my heart, within the heart of the Universe and within the heart of God. I would like to thank my guides, higher beings and God for this meditation, Amen.'

This is the meditation I had done every morning to manifest the £5000 I had needed to save for my recent spiritual adventure. I'd managed to get the money in three months, and it seemed to work perfectly in making me abundant, not just in the financial sense.

I had been waiting for about fifteen minutes, and after I had repeated my mantra I thought, right, I'll put some music on. As I was clumsily untangling my headphones, I heard a beep, and as I looked around, an executive Audi had pulled up on the hard shoulder. I hadn't even had my thumb out.

I bounded in, chucking my bag onto the back seat and jumping in the front.

"Thank you so much. I thought I was going to be there for ages," I said.

"No problem mate, I was stuck there waiting for two hours years ago, with two massive bags of weed in me pockets." Gareth worked for a packaging company.

"With cardboard boxes?" I asked.

"Yes," he replied.

"Funny," I said, "me friend Phil who I'm off to see works with cardboard boxes, you two would have so much to talk about."

He went on to tell me about his two-hour wait that ended in a car screeching to a halt and waving him in. They flung open the doors and were all drinking straight vodka out of the bottle. He jumped in, soon to realise they were joyriding. They dropped him off fifteen miles up the road at a bus stop, giving him the directions to the party they were heading towards.

I told him about my hitching in the US and then he came out with a story about a girl he knew who was hitching in Texas and a guy pulled up in a car and said, "You shouldn't be doing that alone you know, there's some bad guys around here, I'll give you a ride to wherever you wanna go."

She was at first hesitant but then realised it was Kenny Rogers so jumped in and was chauffeur driven by the biggest name in country music, boom, boom, boom.

Gareth decided to go two junctions past his exit to drop me where he thought I would have a better chance of getting a ride. Considering he was on work time, it was no skin off his nose. I thanked him and watched as his fancy company car drove off.

I was at Oxford services and took up a nice little spot leading back onto the M40. I said my mantra again, and my left arm could now operate independently without the two-finger support from the right. Some cars would beep, some people would not even look at me, and occasionally someone would kind of point towards the road in front and shrug their shoulders as if to say "I'm not going that way." I would think, well there is only one way you can go, thus me positioning myself here to avoid any such confusion.

A car pulled up, I grabbed my things, and as I turned it sped away, obviously with its inhabitants thinking it was the funniest thing ever. The immaturity of people in this country who are scared by anyone doing anything different was immediately evident. It's like they felt the need to ridicule people to assure themselves and their peers that they are indeed living the right way, whatever that means.

I got back in position and after fifteen minutes decided it was music time. I put my headphones in, started to listen to Beck and an Audi TT pulled up. I was thinking, is this going to be another joke?, but it stayed and I grabbed my stuff, opened the door, said hello and thanks whilst trying to force my bag into the non-existent back seat. I was now riding in style.

Gavin was a long-haired trade plate driver and was delivering this car to somewhere in Birmingham. He told me about the job, how bad the pay was and that they usually hitched back from a job if there was no car to return in. This was a part of existence I had never known about before, these men all over the country delivering cars whilst we go about our day.

I was dropped at the junction to the A43 towards Northampton, and after walking for a little while I found a spot. Again the cars were going past me so quickly, it was manic. The roundabout that filtered traffic my way was just a constant stream of cars, lorries, vans, caravans and motorbikes. I said my mantra and put my untangled headphones into my ears to muffle out the traffic.

I had been waiting twenty minutes when a little white car stopped. The guy got out, opened the boot and threw my stuff in. Lucas was Polish, I sensed they must be friendly people, and he was also a trade plate driver on his way to Leeds. I told him my plans for the next few days and he said, "Well, I can take you to Leeds now." Sorry Lucas, not part of the plan, even though I was open to just flowing. It did seem appealing to get such a big bit of my journey out of the way in one hit, but I had no reason to go to Leeds, and I seemed to be doing pretty well.

After some chit chat and discovering the dismal wages these people get and the fact he was wanting to save for his wedding, Lucas dropped me off at the side of a roundabout. It was somewhere I would have never stopped, and he tried to cut across three lanes of traffic back onto the roundabout as several cars beeped and shot wanker signs his way before he saw the police and decided it would be better to turn around at the next roundabout 100 meters further along.

I floated away.

I was close to Northampton and started to hitch that way. There was not much action, and the spot where I was standing was a bit blind, and there was no real lay-by.

Phil rang. "You're close mate, I'll come get ya." Result!

I arrived at destination two on my UK tour, pretty chuffed and excited by how the world had helped me out today and some of the good laughs and stories I had shared with my drivers. It was great to see Phil and his daughters. We now just had to wait for me best mate Sally to get home from work, and when she did, we hugged and hugged and hugged.

That evening was spent catching up, and I shared my excitement about everything, my new-found love and want to concentrate on my creative stuff. We went to a funfair that was in town, watching the girls enjoy the gypsy operated (makes you feel sick just looking at) rides. Sally and Phil and the girls all seemed so happy, and the little bubble of life they had was very beautiful.

It was a flying visit, and after big, big loves from Sally the next day, Phil took me to a junction. He was heading to the zoo with his girls so would drop me off at the nearby A1, which would lead me all the way to Newcastle in the northeast and destination three. I looked around, and I realised I had been dropped off at the quietest place imaginable to pick up a ride. There were so few cars in this area, and as I made my way to the entrance to the A1, I thought, this could take a while, but I had said my mantra and meditated that morning, and I said my mantra again and again.

You start to think about odds when you're standing there. A busy area with lots of cars going past and a nice place for them to stop just past you seems ideal. This had a nice place to stop just in front but possibly only a car every minute or so going that way. Still the odds were better than some of the desolate places I had managed to get lifts from in no-man's land in the States.

Seven minutes later, a car pulled up, and I jumped in. Warwick in his little works van introduced himself. He was a calm guy and told me he wasn't going far but would take me to the services nine miles up where I'd have a good chance of getting a lift.

He was a landscape gardener and worked at a lot of little festivals setting up stages and rigs. He dropped me at the services where I saw three motorcycle hearses. Never seen anything like that before; the sidecar carried the coffin, and the bike in a parallel fashion pulled it along. Maybe it was a sign?

"Goodbye Warwick, my saviour, have a great day," blew in the wind as he drove off, gratitude sweeping out of me towards him.

Back to the task at hand, I positioned myself on the downward slope onto the busy A1. There was space just behind me for the car to stop and plenty of time for the passing traffic to see me. The sun was shining as I said my mantra again. I had heard that the weather had been terrible until my arrival back in the UK and it was now perfect for hitching; no rain and some good sun.

As I stood there, I started to learn a new mantra which is what I am supposed to use at the start of me healing sessions. So after 10 or so minutes of standing there and getting a few wanker signs and various levels of abuse, I decided to recite it and start to memorise it:

'I call upon the energy Bagua of the Christ Consciousness and our healing guides to work through my channel bringing love and healing to (the person's name you are healing).' But I added: *'to all those I come in contact with and all those that see me.'*

I said it over and over again trying to get it to stick in my mind. I was smiling my head off singing songs, doing some yoga, having the best time ever and generally loving life and what I was doing. I smiled at every passing car. It was so nice to be in this mood. Cars passed, and waved, wanker signs were thrown and the, 'forward point and shrug I'm not going that way' mystery continued. It was interesting to observe the level of immaturity from the passing cars and vans I interacted with.

Nowhere else in the world had I encountered the slightest bit of abuse. Again phantom rides stopped, and as I picked up my heavy bags and approached the car, they sped off beeping and flashing wanker signs at me. The past me would have become very wound up, angry and given them abuse back and been down on the whole experience, but now I smiled, laughed and put my thumb up to say thanks for getting me closer to my ride. I was buzzing and dancing about. When there was a gap in traffic, I would bend down facing the opposite direction so that when my head was near my knees, I could see any potential lifts upside down. As my body faced the wrong way for the coming traffic, I went into a backbend. It felt so good to stretch. Then when a car came over the brow of the hill, I would flip around and assume my position.

I had been waiting a while, so I thought it was music time. I listened and sang along to two tracks, and as I stood, a car pulled up right beside me pulling a trailer. They didn't pull over onto the hard shoulder which I had neatly prepared in front of me. They just stopped, blocking the lane. Fortunately, there were two lanes, so after a few beeps, cars behind were able to pass. This was to be the theme of my latest ride with this unconventional family. I was about to start an incredible journey.

"Where you off t lad?" a rather chubby-faced, spectacle-wearing, bald chap said. "Newcastle."
"Jump in, fella, take y t Leeds."
"Sweet," I thought.
"Get in lad!" he repeated.

The car was crammed; lady driver, chubby bloke in the front and two teenagers in the back. I squeezed into the one available space, and as I opened the door I was hit by thick smoke. It was like walking into a working man's club before the smoking ban. They all had a lit fag puffing away. Was I getting into a car with the cast of *The Royle Family*?

The family were the Balls; Dad Martin, Mum Michelle and kids Tammy, 16, and Mark, 15. They were from Leeds and had just been to pick up a tricycle ice cream machine and stand which was what the trailer was all about. They worked at festivals, and events doing hamster runs, which I was led to believe are big rubber balls that you run around in. They'd just stopped for a McDonald's breakfast before getting back on the A1. For once I thanked McDonald's for its addictive unhealthy food as it had provided me these characters to observe. Martin was like Jim Royle with big chuckled laughs and constant stories and banter with the kids. Every other word was, 'fuck', 'fucking, 'bastard' or 'twat', but underneath this barrage of abuse they gave each other was a real love — or at least an accepting realisation they were blood and stuck with each other.

They said they hadn't seen anyone hitching for a long time, maybe a year or so was the last time they'd stopped for anyone, but they always did if they had room. Good deeds only reward you with good deeds, said the dad. Wow, was this a man who knew the laws of the Universe, I thought. He was all over Karma.

The kids constantly bickered, which I found hilarious. It was like I was in a car of working-class stereotypes. Everyone was cadging fags off each other and money was being owed and borrowed all the time.

Martin said, "What's Tammy doing over there?" as he pointed to a slag heap at the side of the road. Everyone laughed, and Mark continued the joke further by saying,

"Yeah, you slag" to then receive a punch in the arm. Martin would then get abuse from Tammy, and his walking stick would start being waved about as he tried to turn in his seat as if having some light epileptic fit. Michelle would try to restrain him whilst everyone laughed, and she tried not to crash the car.

There were stories about arrests, Tammy leaving home, work they did for their parents at the festival and the advanced wages they always demanded. I discovered they earn £10 a day for their services. Mark had recently been arrested because Tammy called the police for him beating her up over money owed and her calling a name. The parents laughed in this guttural way as the story was being told as if it was a regular occurrence, with some underlying pride of regular arrests and drama. They all hated the police.

Martin seemed to have had a colourful life. Michelle listened to his stories and nodded away. I was certain she had heard them a thousand times before. One was about his dad, who used to drive the wagons and had taught Martin from a very young age (five) how to drive them. At the age of eight,

Martin could drive one of these massive wagons with these extender peddles his dad had built and would drive part of the journey so his dad could sleep.

This one time he said, "I got int wagon at the yard and me dad went to sleep. I drove the 300 miles south to the destination I knew really well, got out whilst the people at the yard unloaded and then got back in and headed for home. Me dad woke up looked around and said 'How far away are we son?'

'15 miles from home, Dad.'

'Ya bloody what?' said Dad.

'Yeah, I dropped it all off.'

'Well ya better pull over, let me drive rest of the way.'"

I was like, "What really, at eight?"

He said yes, and the kids nodded and said, "Yes, Granddad told us."

I could just imagine Martin as an eight-year-old on a seven-hour round trip in a massive wagon! Mental!

The stories flowed, and the banter was nonstop, if not a little crass, but I adapted and had a great time with the family. I was continually offered fags, and they couldn't grasp the fact that I didn't smoke. If there was a chance of me catching cancer from this influx of passive inhalation it was now.

The traffic was horrendous, and we crawled past a garage. Mark jumped out for energy drinks for the family and much-needed fags. Money was argued about for a while, and finally he was given a tenner to attain the goods. He returned, and straight away, Martin said, "Where's me bloody change you thieving little twat?"

Four hours after being picked up and forgetting what fresh air smelt and tasted like, I jumped out on the A1 somewhere north of Leeds. I gave them a picture from Peru and watched the car leaving a trail of fumes coming out of the window and not the exhaust.

Within 10 minutes of having my thumb out, I was picked up by Zoe and Charlie the dog, a highland terrier who wouldn't give up the front seat. My first female chauffeur and a lovely one at that.

The couple were off to the Lake District camping with some friends and could take me quite a way further up the A1. Zoe said she "often picked up hitchhikers, but you rarely see them anymore." She was amazing, and we had this really intense fast chat about travelling, hitchhiking, food, camping and she wanted to know all about my travels and the eco-house building I had done in the US. I scatted out as much information as I could.

It was a distinct change to what I could discuss with the Balls, where I just generally agreed with everything Martin said and laughed when everyone else did. Zoe told me how her friends think she's mad picking people up and actually hitchhiking herself. She said it's a holiday in itself just hitching around and seeing where you end up.

What a beautiful way to be, I thought, free and unrestricted by time. Flashes of Utopia blinded my vision, my need for slowness, my need to see the bits in-between that people miss by flying and always being pressed for time.

Michael Reynolds' book, The Coming of Wizards, flashed into my mind, and I thought of what he says about us needing to change our concept of time. Most people are dictated to by time. It keeps us all in a rush with no time for anything or being pushed for time. However, it should be our friend and help us be free and flexible and not miss the magic that is always around us. He goes on to talk about how the invention of clocks have made us slaves and given us a dogmatic vision of time in which we are trying to cram more and more into less time and are all rats running around the wheel we call the rat race. Producing more and more products to consume with less and less time to consume them in. When will it stop?

Arrrgh, my head crushed at the thought of this madness and being in a crazy city where this was optimised.

It got me thinking about how I'd started to take the bus to and from London again to see my girlfriend. People thought I was mad for doing so as it takes five hours, as opposed to the two-hour train journey. But my life isn't dictated to by time, and I feel blessed for that. That five hours on the bus was one of the only times I got to submerge myself in a book, catch up with some writing and chill. No one in the rat race can do this as it's far too rigid, and people are less capable of leaning away from their dilemmas because nothing can be done slowly anymore. We are all tied up in so many tangles that to free ourselves would not only be scary but a long, drawn-out process we don't have enough time for.

Being stuck in this system makes it harder and harder to escape...

Zoe's conversation flung my mind all over. She was an amazing girl, very funny with a dry sense of humour and a very clever mind. She booted me out before she turned toward the majestic lakes.

My next position was at a place that lorry drivers stop for a sleep, some kind of lay-by before you join the A1. It was a pretty busy spot. I said my mantras, smiled and assumed my position. The sun was shining, I was getting a little burnt, but I just kept on dancing to the tunes inside my ears, buzzing my tits off at my day so far. I had been standing a while when a lorry pulled up. I grabbed my bags, went to get in and he said, "No mate, I'm just stopping".

Back to my spot, it was, abuse was thrown and caught and returned with a smile. I was at this spot quite a while, maybe thirty minutes or so when a flatbed van pulled up with a massive skinhead bloke in it.

"Throw your stuff on the back, man," he said in a thick Geordie accent (Newcastle language). I flung the heavy bag on the back and jumped in the cab. Gary was a builder from Sunderland, so a Mackum, not a Geordie, and he had done a bit of hitchhiking in his time. He told stories from the early 80s before the mobile and him ending up stuck somewhere and having to hitch home. He said after that he did it quite a bit and it was pretty easy in them days up the A1.

I told him of my travels, and he said, "Oh, I wish I'd done that when I was young like."

I said, "It's never too late man, you can do anything you want at any age, it's just a barrier society creates."

He looked at me dumbfounded, so I panicked and tried to find a comfortable level of conversation. "Do you like football, Gary?" I asked.

"No man, it's a waste of time. I just like me wife, work and me holidays in Spain."

This made me a bit envious of such a simple life, but that was not my path, so I cracked on, thinking about the amazing people I was about to reconnect within Newcastle. He kept apologising he couldn't take me all the way into Newcastle as it was approaching rush hour, but he dropped me off at Sunderland bus stop with directions and details of the £3 fair.

"All the very best to you, Gary, you're a top bloke," bellowed from my lungs as I looked into his eyes.

I got to Newcastle and met the awaiting Mr Horner. Ash (Mr Horner) and I became good friends after he cast me as the lead in his first feature film '*brilliantlove*'. His friendly face whisked me off to his house to be reacquainted with his wife Rowen and little boy Moss. It was a lad's night at the cabin, so we took the 15-minute drive into the beautiful Northumberland countryside to Ash's latest acquisition, 'a shack in the woods'.

It's amazing how fast you can get from the centre of Newcastle to pure wilderness. The shack was built in the late 1800s and is said to have been lived in by a priest for some time. It has no mains connection, and the water is collected and pumped in, so for the night, we were real men.

There is a little river at the end of the garden that leads to the River Tyne. It has this small kitchen leading to the living room, which is like something from *The Hobbit* or *Harry Potter*. The bedroom has these ornately made double bunk beds.

Ashley serenaded me with his ukulele; we fantasised about having property abroad and hit the sack.

The next morning, Ash wanted to shoot his lunch, so after him trying to shoot things for a while unsuccessfully and trying to catch some fish with Moss, we headed back to his casa. Maybe my vegetarian vibes had pre-informed the animals that carnivores were on the prowl for dinner.

That evening, two of my favourite people arrived for dinner, Karl and the goddess that is Joy Sanders. The way she glides into a room takes your breath away. Her glowing blue eyes could melt the hardest of men. It becomes difficult to take your eyes off her, but with that being deemed inappropriate in a social setting, I made a decision to sit next to her at dinner so I couldn't stare too much.

The way she speaks is like a Japanese silk dancer draping her silks around your head and body. When her words float over and touch you, your mind absorbs their deep resonance as if a flash of divinity is soothing your soul. She is like that enigmatic person in a band or a play you can't take your eyes off, and you don't know why, it's just something they have, that sparkle, that shine, that otherworldly majesty.

Karl is my homeboy, he produced '*brilliantlove*'. After we ate, we had good time chats about London-bound lives for us both, hanging out down there and on the differing stages of our relationships. We all hung out in the living room chatting, playing guitar and listening to Ash's tales.

Rowan, Ash's wife, is a burlesque dancer, and she showed us some of her latest work, which was mildly provocative in an arty, sophisticated way. I loved being in Ash and Rowan's home, it was so liberating and dysfunctional in a poetically functional way. Somewhere that inspires, somewhere that provides comfort and is full of loving creativity. I didn't want to leave.

The next day we woke, and all had a cup of tea in the main bed of the house. We all chilled out in Mummy and Daddy Bears' bed, then Ash made food. Rowan and I exchanged therapies in the garden, I did some healing on her fragile back, and I got a shiatsu massage. We ate, had a quick photoshoot in the front garden and then Ash dropped me off at the start of the A69 heading toward Carlisle, leading to my next stop, Glasgow, and the exquisite Macbeth-Malyon family.

Mantra had been said, and I prayed to get to exactly where I needed and to spread some cheer on the way. I was positioned just in front of a bus stop so my ride would have to pull up there. I realised when the bus was there my pursuit was redundant, so I just smiled. My posture was really there now, the stance was perfect, and it would only be a matter of time before someone stopped for me.

No one did. It had been twenty-five minutes.

I said all my mantras again, started to put on my music and as I did that, Fhian called. I got some mild abuse as we chatted, which I waved back at regally. I had to cut my call short as my ride arrived. "Bye-bye baby," as I fumbled into the car.

The seat was flipped down, and I was thrown in the back.

"Say hello to Kevin and JoJo. I haven't picked one up for years," she said to Kevin as I got in as if I were a specific breed of something. It kind of made me feel special.

Kevin was a landscape gardener just about to move to the Midlands, JoJo worked in the music industry for a label in Newcastle. She knew Pinball films, and I told her I was in one of their movies. We chatted music and film, and I wanted to stay and just chat, but I had to keep moving as Glasgow was far. I gave her my card, and I heard from Karl a few days later that she had emailed him saying "I think we picked your mate up the other day, interesting lad, definitely got the stories you need from someone you give a ride to."

She asked if I made it and Karl told her yes, they then chatted about work and about the possibility of working together in the future in music or film. Amazing! She also told him I have a very peaceful aura and it was a pleasure to give me a ride. I would like to thank my aura for glowing so vibrantly and attracting these amazing souls.

I was further along the A69. They wanted to take me all the way, but they had stuff to do. I got a nice little spot, said my mantras and prayers and waited.

After 10 minutes on the quiet road, I fumbled for the headphones. As I looked up, a small estate van pulled up. I was starting to think that maybe going for the music was some kind of lucky ritual, or someone did not want me to listen to Beck. I peered in, and this massive skinhead bloke was sitting there, wearing a vest with tattoos on his arms. What you may describe as a mother's worst nightmare. I went for it, knowing it was all cool.

"Thanks so much for the ride man, where you heading?"

"Carlisle."

'Amazing,' I thought as I smiled.

Mark was delivering some ice-branding equipment. He talked of his love of driving on the open road all over the country, especially the north and Scotland. The views we passed were getting more and more spectacular, and he told me of this place in Scotland where the road looks like you're going downhill, but you're actually going up, and how it was something to do with the Earth's magnetic force at that point.

He then told me of the places he had lived, the 10 kids him and his partner had between them and how much he loved them all. I said I was a bit jealous as that was all I wanted now and couldn't wait to get started. He had a real love for the Irish and was impressed with me being half that way inclined.

He told me how he used to hitchhike 70 minutes outside of Belfast and back every day from work and how there was never a day he was late or didn't manage to get home. He did this for 18 months.

We got on to my travels, and I told him how it had been a bit of a spiritual pursuit for me.

He said, "I never believed in any of that stuff till the other year when I was in Benidorm on me holidays, and I went to this church up the hill. As I was sat in there, something really strange happened. All these weird feelings started, and I could feel me mother. I just broke down crying and sobbed for about an hour. I couldn't stop, and the missus thought I was going mental or something. Since then I have felt a lot of things, and lots of weird things I can't explain have happened."

We got into life after death and spirits and all the things we can't see, and for about an hour, we had one of the deepest chats I had ever had in my life, with a man I'd thought could possibly murder me when I'd first looked into his car.

We got to Gretna Green where he was dropping me. I just wanted to stay and explore this gentle giant's soul more, but we both had to leave. We had a cuddle in the van, and I told him he was amazing, and that was it, an Angel, gone.

I couldn't believe it again, my misconceptions and stereotypes were shattered. I was learning to try and see inside people, not what they portray in our image-conscious society, and my pre-programmed dogmatic attitude towards appearances, but it seemed a hard habit to break.

Touched and amazing after my latest chariot disappeared over the horizon, I assumed my position at the Gretna Green services trying to get to Glasgow on the A74. It was such a funny experience watching foreign cars dither around the roundabout and then make their way onto the slip road to discover they had gone wrong and then start to reverse. Luckily it wasn't that busy, and there was a lazy Sunday feel in the air. At one point, one of these mistaken families pulled up in front of me. I did my usual thing and tried to get in, but they waved no, "We just got lost."

"Okay sorry," I said, as they unconfidently and dangerously reversed.

It had been about twenty-five minutes, so I got out the headphones. On my second Beck track, Ian pulled up in a Ford Transit. He was heading north of Glasgow, so I was almost there. Ian was this amazing softly spoken guy from somewhere near Portsmouth. He was a cute little man with mousy blond red hair and freckles all over his face. I wanted to cuddle him. He'd had an amazing life, heading over to France with £20 in his pocket at the age of 17 and coming back thirty years later with a wife, three kids and quite a bit of cash. He had hitchhiked all through France picking up the language as life took him from place to place. He said he was given places to stay, money and even a job from people who'd picked him up.

He was off to Lochgolihead an hour north of Glasgow, which was on a crystal clear lake that shimmered in the moonlight. It sounded magical, and he was currently living between there and the south coast. He told me about him and his friends doing the Mongal rally last year, driving from London to Mongolia to raise money for charity.

He asked where I was going in Glasgow, I said, "East end, I think."

"What's the postcode?" he said.

I gave it to him, and he tapped it into the satnav.

I said, "No, don't worry about that, I'll jump out anywhere, I don't want to take you out of your way."

He insisted and took me to the door, what a guy. Again I felt massively blessed. I thought what a great end to a magical day. Ian headed for Lochgolihead after his massive detour, and I thanked him and everyone for getting me here.

Now it was Molly time, babies were to be a theme for the next few days.

Tie, Justin and Molly live in a tenement block in Dennistoun on the east side of Glasgow. Architecturally the buildings are beautiful, with large terracotta sandstone blocks covering the exterior and beautiful imposing bay windows. When you enter, ornate features cascade around the staircase and stained-glass windows on each little landing look out to the central gardens, giving it this feeling of grandeur. The quality of buildings that used to be built to house workers was just amazing. They were built in the early 1900s and are still standing strong.

When you look at the paper-thin walls in the made-to-look-swanky apartments being built to house workers these days, (yes you may wear a tie and work in an office but you are a modern-day factory or dock worker, end of) you can't imagine any of them still standing in 50 years, let alone 100. These buildings are actually only being built to last 25 years so the machine that is the economy can keep being oiled, fact.

Tie and Molly awaited me, and we spent time catching up before we headed for the park. It was the first time I had been to Glasgow, and the sun was out. It was so nice to see one of my best mates and her little girl. Molly had gotten so big since I'd seen her last. Tie was the first one of my uni mates to have a baby, and I hoped it would start a craze. I thought babies were cool.

Justin arrived at the park, and we practised handstands and yoga poses, attracting a bit of attention from Tenants' super-drinking crack heads. I felt at home with Tie and her family. It was so good to see what they had created. It confirmed all I wanted that contentedness it had given them both and the love they all had for each other. It felt a far cry from our intoxicated raving and partying days.

The next evening was more baby time. I'd recently found out my niece Kay had moved just outside Glasgow with her husband Sam and two daughters, Poppy and Grace. So I headed there. I spent some time in a small tent and then chalked some walls, and I felt a young Banksy may be forming in Grace. I think someone was sick on me at one point and then we ate and I read Grace a bedtime story.

I woke to being jumped on in the morning and spent time playing with the girls. We headed to the park to meet Tie and witness baby bonding. The sun was still out and, creamed up, we all chilled in the park.

The next morning, I headed out. My next stop was Lancaster and a meeting with the one and only Mr Wiggins. It was farewell to all the babies and friends, and I was broodier than ever.

From Tie and Justin's house, it was a mile or so walk to a motorway. The entrance to the motorway was quiet, and again the sun was shining. The travelling vest man had said all his mantras and even done some yoga that morning, so I was ready for my people. No one was pulling over. Car after car passed and just as I was going for my earphones, Martin from just outside Glasgow stopped. Without pulling over into the lay-by.

I positioned myself in front of Martin, who was blocking traffic. Eventually, after figuring out he could give me a lift, he pulled over. The car was a bit scruffy, a really small three-door. As I was about to get in, I realised another car had pulled up behind, and the driver at the helm was wearing a black and white collar. A man of the cloth, I thought. Interesting, this could be a sign, but I had committed to Martin, and I was getting in. He had a thick Glaswegian accent that I could only just about understand, it was almost like a slur. Unfortunately, he wasn't going far, and I was dropped off a few junctions down.

I then realised the junction back on to the motorway was blocked, it looked like it hadn't been used for a while. I then realised I had to walk two miles with all my stuff to get to a place I could hitch from. Should have gone with the man of the cloth, I thought. But maybe it was a disguise, and Martin had actually saved my life?

The heat was beating down, and I was sweaty. I'd never imagined Scotland could get so hot.

I arrived at my spot, which was on a big bend, and the traffic was hitting 50 miles an hour as it passed. The sun was intense; I was getting burnt. No one was stopping, and I was getting my usual abuse. Then I got a phantom stopper who was filming as I picked up my bag and raced towards them to only see them pull off at speed. Should search for that on Youtube maybe? The forward nod point and shrug continued, mainly from lorry drivers. Maybe it's a code?

I was waiting there for a long time. I was thinking maybe I should try another spot, but there was nowhere. I got through one Beck album, then another. I had been waiting over an hour, more than double the amount of time I had waited anywhere else. Whilst accessing my current predicament, I realised that you can sometimes be waiting all day and that to wait three hours isn't that unusual, so I was actually in a fortunate position.

It was so hot and almost midday. The plan was to meet Mr Wiggins just outside Lancaster after he finished school. I tried yoga, my mantras, smiling, praying, and turning my music on and off, nothing was working. Then 20 minutes later, a little car pulled up, and I jumped in. Elaine was driving, a young round-faced girl with quite a few tattoos and piercings. She said she would just drop me off at the next services. We chatted music and festivals, and before I knew it, I was waiting in a nice spot leading from Glasgow services on to the M74.

I had this nice grassed area to stretch out on, but before I knew it a van stopped and I was off again. Steve and his son Mark were from Leeds and were delivering furniture up and down the country to care homes for the elderly. They could take me as far as Penrith. It wasn't far to Mr Wiggins from there.

It was a couple of hours' trip, so I tried to sit back and chill, but Steve's chat was constant and a stream of stories about scuba diving and all the equipment needed. His experiences picking up hitchhikers poured out, some of which he'd had to kick out because they were rude and unappreciative. He also told me about the trips him and his family and some friends had taken to Spain and Italy, driving down in their cars and doing bumps of speed so they could do the gruelling 20-hour drive in one hit. Bumping speed whilst driving seemed to be a bit of a theme for Steve and I was just imaging him buzzing his nut off as his oblivious family tried to relax whilst he was gurning to some Old Skool classics.

Steve and Mark headed east on the A66, and I joined the slip road to the M6. Not long after I was picked up by a little van. John was driving, he was a tall bloke and did some kind of engineering work, and by the look of him, could potentially kidnap people and bury them in the Dales. I discovered he was from Offerton in Stockport, which is only a couple of miles from the area I class as home. It was tempting, but I had plans, and I was going to stick to them. I told him about my travels and what I had been up to. He told me about the troubles of teenage kids and the difficulties of drunken pickups and sleepless nights when they don't return till late. He told me about his son being in a band and my ears pricked up. He said he has a CD and I told him to stick it on. I think he was a little bit embarrassed and didn't think I would like it, but they were pretty good.

We stopped at the services, and he made me a brew in the back of his van before kindly taking a detour and dropping me off where Mr Wiggins would be picking me up.

I was early for Mr Wiggins, so I sat in the shade on the grass verge of the Hilton Hotel awaiting his arrival. I started to reminisce about how I'd met this lovely little combover man. In 2006 at a music festival in Spain, he was walking back to the campsite off his nut with a Japanese bloke whose foot wasn't in his shoe properly. My friend Absy, being a stereotypical British gent, thought this inappropriate and painful-looking, so stopped the chaps and put the Japanese man's foot back in his shoe properly. A friendship was born and ever since we have kept in contact and been away together a few times.

Mr Wiggins arrived in his new flashy head of PE and Year 8 car and we rekindled a friendship that has always been strong, with a massive embrace and then some piss-taking.

His flat overlooks Morecambe Bay, and in the distance, the hills and mountains of the Lake District puncture the skyline. It's such an amazing view. Unfortunately, it is obscured by the Polo Tower that was a ride at the famous Frontier Land which has been derelict for over a decade. The upside is that from Mr Wiggins's bed you can give yourself a Green and Blue Polo erection if you lay flat as it juts and breaks the skyline. I lay there for a while revelling in the childish delight of having a huge packet of

Polos for a penis. I really hope I'm still buzzing off that kind of stuff when I'm 80. Me dad is in his seventies, and he still does.

The next day, after a morning run along the promenade, I had a photoshoot with a photographer, who is actually the mother of the awkward foot-out-of-shoe Japanese bloke's daughter. We shot in the most beautiful location called Sham Beach on the rocks looking out to the bay as the sun-blessed us by not being blocked by clouds, or maybe the clouds blessed us by not being around?

Soon after this, the photographer Sarah messaged me saying there was something really strange on one of the pictures, and that after taking thousands and thousands of pictures she had never seen anything like it before. It looks to me like an angel or a fairy inside a diamond filled with amazing purple light is sitting just above my head. I really wish I knew what it was and what it actually signified. Maybe I'll find out when I leave this body?

That evening after Mr Wiggins finished work we hit the gym, and I hadn't lost it. Then we headed for some food, and I met his beautiful new lady, Miss Fish, who we had a little walk around Lancaster with. I discovered she lived on this cobbled street in a lovely little terraced house. Then I was shown a statue of Queen Victoria that, when viewed from a certain angle, looks like she is holding a massive cock. I was in tears of laughter again.

The next morning, the final leg of my journey began. I was going home after eight months away, to see my dad and some family, re-acquaint with friends and for the first time, think about what I was going to do with myself.

Mr Wiggins dropped me off on his way to school at 8am at an entrance to the M6. I made my way onto the slip road. There wasn't really anywhere to stand as I walked along the grass verge. Cars beeped at me as if to say, 'Where are you going you, nutter?' The now-experienced left thumb revealed itself to the passing traffic. There was only one lane, and the traffic was all coming off traffic lights at the bottom junction. I realised it was really only the last car that had the possibility of stopping for me without causing a major accident. So I walked a bit further and was now practically on the motorway. I realised this was a bad idea and I could possibly be arrested, if not killed. I decided to make my way back to the road and reduce my possible escorts by 50% by standing near the traffic lights turning left onto the motorway and missing the traffic turning right.

After two minutes, I was picked up by Simon, who could drop me at the services 20 minutes away before he turned off. He told me tales of waiting for three hours quite a few times when he was hitching. He asked me how long I had been waiting.

"Two minutes mate, sorry!"

Next was a four-minute wait before Emma, Ben, Elka and Amber picked me up (Elka and Amber being dogs, a lurcher and a labrador). The lovely couple were from Kendal (what a lovely place to be from, I thought) and they now lived in Edinburgh (what a lovely place to live, I thought). They were off to visit a sister in Wigan (Wigan, I thought). Ben told me of his hitchhiking exploits and how once he'd gotten into someone's car who had stopped and was promptly told to get out as they'd just stopped to take a phone call.

We chatted about our travels. A few years ago Ben had cycled through Peru on a trip from Argentina to Mexico and I was very impressed. Emma used to live in Chorlton, which is the coolest part of Manchester, and she used to work in my favourite supermarket in the world, 'Unicorn', the only vegan one around. I love that place. I can go in there and not think about where something is from or if it has bad stuff in; that has already been done for me. Sadly they couldn't take me too far, as I could have sat and chatted with them for hours.

They dropped me at some services before the turnoff for Wigan. I stood and waited, thumb out. Within two minutes a car stopped, it was a small Vauxhall thing. Four young guys were inside, and the driver shouted, "Where you going?"

I instantly thought they were going to do a hit-and-run on me, and as I gathered my bags, drive off.

"Manchester," I replied.

"Well, we can drop you off on the M6 somewhere."

They were all laughing, and I was paranoid as I approached. He had now pulled his seat forward, enticing me into the back. I asked if I could put my bag in the boot.

"No, it's full," was the response I got, "put it on the back shelf."

The back shelf was the size of an A4 piece of paper. I squeezed my body into the only available space. Two boys were smoking and rolling joints as I clambered in, my small bag went between my legs and my massive rucksack on me knee.

I was in. It was not a hoax or a joke, but now I found myself in this surreal world at 9:15am on a Thursday morning. All the boys seemed either very drunk, massively excited or just straight mental.

Before I knew it, I was being offered a joint, "No, thanks."

"Would you like a pill?"

"No, mate."

"Some MDMA."

"No mate, I've not seen me dad for eight months, and I don't want to turn up off me nut." Refraining from telling them I no longer participate in such practices of enjoyment, trying to keep an element of credibility with these hectic youths. They were from Chorley, I instantly thought of Chorley FM, 'coming in your ears', a Peter Kay catchphrase. Drugs, drink and laughter were very much in abundance, and I was like, "Where are you guys going? Why do you have so many drugs?"

"We're going to see the Stone Roses in Finsbury Park, we've got backstage passes, and you're coming as well, we've got a spare ticket."

"I can't, boys, I'm going to see me dad and me sister, not seen them for eight months!"

"No, you're not mate, how you gonna get out? We're kidnapping you."

They were all laughing. I was unsure of the severity of their threat. At most other stages of my life, this would have seemed like an amazing opportunity, but now it seemed like my worst nightmare. Part of me wanted to go and laugh, have a weirder story to tell, observe these guys for the day and watch a band I'd loved when I was younger. We all laughed, and I hoped that meant it was a joke.

I was in a car with Louis, Callum, Tom and Jack. Tom, who was sitting next to me, told me he had crashed his car that morning drunk and that for some reason he had put the excess at £2000 on his policy. So he was going to be skint for a long time. There were stories of drugs, fights, crazy parties and the usual stuff lads get involved in, from these areas. Bigger and bigger bags of drugs were being flashed in front of me, trying to entice me in with different and weirder concoctions. Was this the final test of my resolve? Was I going to succumb? No, I had no interest in getting high before meeting my family again, if I was definitely being kidnapped then maybe. The boys wanted to know what I did. I thought of telling them a few things; healer, spiritual seeker, yoga enthusiast, and eco-house builder. I told them none of the above and decided to go with actor and window fitter. They still thought I was gay.

We missed my exit, and I was half thinking they were actually kidnapping me before we pulled off at the next one, and they let me out. I wished them a great time, but with the amount of drugs they had, how could they not?

I was safe, I was not going to London, even though it would have meant I could have felt Fhian again. Alas, I had an itinerary I wanted to stick to and set in stone dates for this UK tour of which Manchester was my final show.

I crossed the overpass and thumbed back towards where I was heading. Unknown to me, this was to be a massive spanner in the works, and the flow of my journey had been affected massively.

A car pulled up, it was a top of the range executive Jaguar. As I approached, I was wondering if this guy had stopped for a reason other than to pick me up. But no, Nige said hello. He was nicely wearing a suit to match the car and said, "Throw your bag in the back."

Looking at the cream leather and the state of me and the luggage I was carrying, I thought, are you sure? But I just did it. Again, I was with an amazing person, he only took me five minutes down the road, but this Scottish man was really cool and obviously really rich, but fair play to him picking up a dishevelled traveller.

Now I was at Knutsford services, about 8 miles from where I wanted to be, the sun was beating down again, and I tried to imagine the last time I returned to Manchester, and there was sun. Maybe never! After a couple of failed attempts to hitch on the M56 slip road, I decided I would hitch to Knutsford and get the train or put me dad on imminent arrival notice and have him come get me.

I'd been making such good time; it was still only 10:30am, but it took a long while to get a lift towards Knutsford.

Finally, this sports BMW pulled up. I thought, are you sure? I said, "I just want to get to Knutsford train station."

He nodded.

I pulled the seat back and put my bag in the back, shut the door and was injected into a racecar world. This bloke, who must have been in his mid-fifties, put his foot to the floor. I was pinned to my seat, going down this country road at about 70, overtaking cars, lorries and tractors. I said, "Thanks for picking me up, how has your day been so far?"

He just looked forward.

I said, "What's your name?"

He just looked forward.

"Where you from?"

He just looked forward. I started to feel really uncomfortable. Why had this guy picked me up?

Sternly he just looked ahead. I wanted to get out, and when I recognised a place, I said,

"Oh this is fine; I can get out here." I got out of this madman's play car and rang me dad. "Come get me, Dad."

"Can't you get a lift?" he said, not wanting to drive the 20 minutes to get me, moaning and me thinking, all I have heard from people is "your dad's really missing you and wants you back." Here I was eight miles away from a father and son embrace, and he didn't want to drive 20 minutes away from watching TV and possibly doing Sudokos. Nothing changes with my old man, he's a law unto himself. I will never understand him. His actions seem to always contradict his true feelings. He's my official idiot, and I love my official idiot.

He arrived in his clapped-out Proton after lots of moaning, missing the turn-in and instead of pulling onto the curb. He jutted across a lane of traffic, blocking all around him in his typical way with no regard whatsoever for social order. I embarrassingly (as has been the way most of my life) covered my head and got into the car.

I was home, back in Manchester where it all began. Nothing had changed, everyone seemed a little angry as usual, and I had been catapulted into the constant dramas of my family members. Was this love and joy I had been carrying around going to be slowly chipped away? I didn't think so. I had my head and heart firmly set on Fhian, on our life together, on concentrating on my creative side and on trying to unleash its full power. Now I was going to have to think about what I was going to do. I knew I wanted to build a house, have my roots so that my future would be more stable. How I was going to achieve that I had no idea, but I knew the Universe would show me the signs.

    I'd done it. I had hitchhiked to get myself to the places I wanted to go. To see the people, I wanted to see. Hitchhiking was not a dead art. It was fully alive. I had put my faith in humanity, and it hadn't let me down. I trusted that everything would be fine and everything was fine. I saw the kindness and generosity strangers can give you if you open up and show a little venerability. There are people out there who want to help you and people who want to spread joy. I felt truly blessed by all the people who had welcomed me so warmly into their space and into their heart. If you trust, everything you want and need will be provided. You just have to believe.

Hi

Thank you so much for purchasing me book! I hope you have enjoyed reading it as much as I have enjoyed sharing my adventure with you. I really truly value you as a reader.

I'd love to hear your feedback on how you feel about the book. If you could take a few minutes to leave a review, I'd be so happy.

To submit your review, simply click below and let me know what you think!

https://www.amazon.co.uk/dp/B0813LJCYR

Thanks in advance for taking the time to leave a review! Feel free to contact me at any time.

liam@liambrowne.com

Cheers,

Liam

This story, and my hitchhiking experiences on my travels inspired a song called 'Hitchin'

Check it out on YouTube: https://youtu.be/Z7bA2i_h5bQ

A FREE 'UNPUBLISHED' POEM FOR YOU!

As a massive thank you for buying this book I would like to give you a little present. This is only for you, the people who have supported my work. I hope my experience has opened your mind to trying things you thought were not possible.

This is a poem about perception and social conditioning. A poem about drugs and alcohol and dogma. A poem about doing what feels right in your heart and not what other people and organisations say is right for you. Steps into your own power. Be all that you can be!

Magnificence is waiting around the corner. Move beyond you imagined limitations.

You can download 'DEALER WITH IT' here:
www.liambrowne.com/dealerwithit

ACKNOWLEDGEMENTS
&
GRATITUDE

First and foremost, all the epic humans (except the weird dude at the end) for picking me up and allowing me into your space. It takes a lot to be so open and trustworthy, allowing a stranger into your car. I respect and honour you all from the bottom of my heart. It was an amazing experience. Massive thanks to all my spiritual teachers over the last 8 years; I owe you all my life. For my Mum for giving me this big heart that can connect with so many people. Thank you to Lady Ayahuasca for teaching me to trust, teaching me to know I am always supported and teaching me to keep having fun and expressing myself. Thank you to all the characters I met on my journey, you will always be family. To each person who listened to my stories and said you must write a book. You are the inspiration. To Keith the Cacao Sharman, Otillia the Ayahuascero for connecting me deeper to my heart. To my editor Johanna, thank you for bringing it all into view. To my art designer Matt Crump, your talent always astounds me. Paulo for creating the cover you are exceptional. Evelyn for your studious eye, final touches and guidance I am again truly blessed to have you.

Finally, to you the readers, more than anything I hope that something in this book can help you find that inner power to do something that allows you to step out of your comfort zone. That makes you want to explore and can give you that confidence to be brave and fearless. Make positive change and to continue to look for growth in all corners of your life. Spread love and healing far and wide. I want to help as many people as humanly possible to step into their power and remove the fear that is blocking them from becoming their finest self. We can all do it; we just have to be willing to work at it. Good luck to you all. FULL POWER!!!!!!!

Now sign up to me mailing list immediately! Please! That would be awesome.

Sing up here Here - www.liambrowne.com

ALSO BY LIAM BROWNE

Books

Dealer to Healer - A Modern Tale of A Fucked Up Male

Short Stories

Hitchhiking - Feel The Good Vibrations

Poetry

Dealer Forget, Healer Remember

LINKS

Everything Liam Browne related and all my social media links can be found via my website. My Podcast 'Dealer to Healer' can be found where ever you listen to your podcasts and on the 'Dealer to Healer' YouTube channel. Please listen and subscribe. Thank you so much for your support.

www.liambrowne.com

Printed in Great Britain
by Amazon